French Jewish Genealogy

from

The French Genealogy Blog

by
Anne Morddel

Suggested cataloguing:

Morddel, Anne

French Jewish Genealogy From the French Genealogy Blog. First Edition

Summary: Guide to researching French Jewish ancestors using French resources.

[1. Genealogy. 2. France – History]

ISBN: 979-10-96085-10-1

Table of Contents

Ancien régime Geography Is Important

When researching Jewish genealogy before the French Revolution, the reach back into the past is long, well into the Medieval era. Borders were different then and France looked quite different, not at all like the "Hexagon" (above) of today. Prior to the final expulsion of 1394, Jewish people were permitted to live only in specific places. These might have been certain towns, within which they may have been limited to just a few streets for residence and work. They endured long years of persecution and previous expulsions, but lived throughout France. It is important to note that, in 1394, the country looked more like this:

Quite a bit less than modern France:

This makes the next map, claiming to show French Jewish communities at the time of the expulsion, quite misleading, as a significant few of those supposedly French Jewish communities were not within the France of that day.

The expulsion, in all its horror, was successful, in that very few Jewish families remained in what was then France. However, their communities just outside of France did survive, as can be seen in the following map.

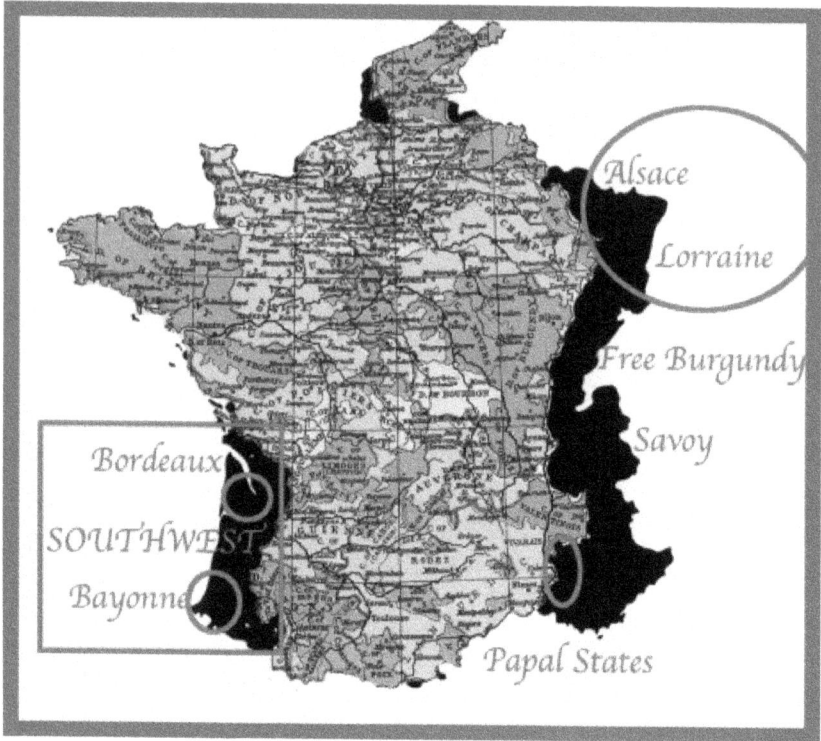

If you are working with only a modern map of France, you will have the impression that the three main areas of Jewish communities:

- The Southwest
- Alsace-Lorraine
- The Papal States and Provence

survived the expulsion *within* France. That would be wrong, because they were not within France at the time of the expulsion and so, if this is not putting too fine a point on it, were Jewish, of course, but not French. The darker shaded areas in the map just above were controlled by other powers:

- By the English in the far northwest and the southwest region of Aquitaine
- A tiny bit in the south belonged to the Kingdom of Navarre
- The Holy Roman Empire held the northeast
- Free Burgundy, Savoy and the Papal States owned all the rest of what is now eastern France

Paris, as ever, was a special case. Though no Jewish people were supposed to be living there, most likely they were. Robert Anchell, in his fascinating article on "The Early History of the Jewish Quarters in Paris", maintains that it is unlikely that Jewish people were ever, at any time since the Medieval Era, absent from Paris. He points out that they certainly must have been very discrete, for there is almost no documentation of Jewish people in Paris for nearly 300 years after the expulsion.

For research purposes, in each of the three main regions of Jewish communities there were different laws, rules, languages, customs and attitudes, making for different search methodologies today. Firstly, the language differences:

- The Southwest, received many refugees from the expulsion of Jewish people from Spain in 1492 and from Portugal in 1497, so many of the surviving documents of the region are in Spanish
- Alsace was part of the Holy Roman Empire for eight hundred years, while Lorraine was an independent duchy that was then governed by Stanislas of Poland. In both regions, the documentation is as much in German and Latin as in French.

- The Papal States or Comtat Venaissin, did not become a part of France until 1791, but Provence was annexed in 1481. The documentation can be in French or Latin

In all locations Jewish documents may also be in Hebrew.

The regions were distinctly different in their treatment of Jewish people in other ways. The Jewish communities also were quite different.

In the Southwest, the Jewish people were almost exclusively Sephardim, from Spain and Portugal, arriving after the expulsions from those countries at the end of the 1400s. For some reason, all usually were termed "Portuguese". They went primarily to the areas in and around Bayonne, just over the border, and Bordeaux, cities that had been annexed by France only forty years earlier. In 1550, the French King Henri II gave full rights to the Bordeaux Jewish arrivals with letters patent, which went specifically to twenty-six merchant families, giving them significant advantages. Bordeaux Jewish families developed businesses in shipping, insurance, banking and the slave trade. They were also quite involved in trade with the French colonies. Silvia Marzagalli writes :

> "In fact, they essentially enjoyed the same rights as a native Frenchman. They could also obtain French naturalization, as well as the title of bourgeois de Bordeaux, which implied several further commercial privileges. ......

> "These measures pertained, however, only to those Portuguese immigrants considered New Christians, that is to say Catholics. This distinction explains why, until the eighteenth century, there was apparently no contradiction between, on the one hand, the various orders expelling

Jews from Bordeaux, and on the other, the ordinances protecting Portuguese merchants: French authorities pretended or assumed that the latter were in fact Christians......."

Thus they were officially tolerated and had formed their own community. no other Jewish group in France would receive these rights.[1]

In Bayonne,[2] Jewish people were not allowed to live in the city itself. They lived primarily in the nearby towns of Saint-Esprit, La Bastide-Clairence, and Peyrehorade but also in many of the small villages of the area. They were served religiously by itinerant rabbis, some of whose records have survived. The communities in this area now straddle the border between two departments, Landes and Pyrénées-Atlantiques, making research a bit more laborious.

In the Papal States and Provence, the towns where Jewish people were permitted to live were:

- Avignon
- l'Isle-sur-la-Sorgue
- Carpentras (which has the oldest continuously functioning synagogue in France and also the oldest Jewish cemetery of the region)
- Cavaillon

However, they were confined to *carrières*, or ghettos. These had gates that were locked at night. The nearby Principality of

[1] Silvia Marzagalli, "Atlantic Trade and Sephardim Merchants in Eighteenth Century France, the Case of Bordeaux" in Paolo Bernardini and Norman Fiering, editors, The Jews and the Expansion of Europe to the West, 1493 -1800. Providence, R.I. : Berghahn Books, 2001.

[2] The finest resource on this group is Léon's Histoire des Juifs de Bayonne, published in 1893.

Orange, which struggled to remain free of France for centuries, came under French rule in 1702, gave Jewish people greater freedom while independent, and became more oppressive afterward.

The region of Alsace-Lorraine, in eastern France, on the modern border with Germany, is historically unique, with unique Jewish communities. The two regions themselves are quite different and it is unfortunate that, in modern history, they have been lumped together as one, for that obscures the differences that are important to the researcher.

Over a long period, beginning in 1552, the Duchy of Lorraine was gradually annexed by France. In the mid-eighteenth century, it was ruled by Stanislaus of Poland but in 1766, was annexed in full to France. Just over a hundred years later, it was annexed by Germany as a prize of the Franco-Prussian War. When Germany was defeated in World War One, Lorraine returned to France in 1918. When Germany invaded France in 1940, the region was annexed to her again, until 1944, when Lorraine returned to France.

During all of this time, the treatment of Jewish people in Lorraine slowly worsened. In 1618, Jewish families were permitted to live in Metz and a synagogue was built there. In Nancy, Jewish people were officially accepted and could live there from 1721. With the annexation by France, these rights were rescinded.

Alsace had been a part of the Holy Roman Empire for eight hundred years and the people were German-speaking and a lived under Holy Roman laws. Jewish people had relative freedom in the countryside but were not allowed to live in the cities of Strasbourg or Colmar. Comparing the two regions, it can be seen why Jewish families from Alsace tended to be farmers, but those from Lorraine tended to have more the professions one finds in cities, an important point to bear in mind when researching your ancestors from this region.

For each of these regions, some of the best research may be done at the relevant Departmental and Municipal Archives. Some of these have been uploading onto their websites some very interesting Jewish materials. These are the departmental and municipal archives relevant to the specific regions:

Southwest:
- Departmental Archives: Landes, Gironde, Pyrénées Atlantiques
- Municipal Archives: Bayonne, Bordeaux

Lorraine:
- Departmental Archives: Moselle, Meurthe-et-Moselle, Meuse, Vosges
- Municipal Archives: Metz, Nancy

Alsace:
- Departmental Archives: Bas-Rhin, Haut-Rhin
- Municipal Archives: Strasbourg, Mulhouse, Colmar

Papal States / Comtat Venaissin:
- Departmental Archives: Vaucluse
- Municipal Archives: Nîmes

Go to The French Genealogy Blog for the up-to-date links to all of the above (in the left-hand column of the blog).

There were other regions where Jewish people did live in France in the period from the 1394 expulsion to the Revolution beginning in 1789. Even though, legally, Jewish people were not permitted to live in Paris, some did so. They were mostly migrants from one of the above three major regions. From at least 1770, there was an Oratory at the Cemetery of Saint-André-des-Arts; it was not a synagogue but a place to worship legally, and was permitted mainly for "Portuguese" Jewish, from Bordeaux, who, with their exceptional rights and, in some cases, even French nationality, were permitted to live in Paris. By the time of the Revolution, approximately five hundred Jewish people lived in Paris.

In Rouen and Nantes, both busy ports, some Jewish merchants from Bordeaux could be found. As in Paris, they tended to be from Bordeaux, with exceptional rights and permitted to operate their businesses. In Toulouse, however, a small community of Jewish people who had been living there for more than six hundred fifty years all were murdered in 1686. The Comté de Savoie and Nice were not a part of France until 1860 and, initially, some Jewish people went there when expelled from France. But those regions also persecuted Jewish people until almost none remained by sixteenth century. For the genealogist, the records of these persecutions, if one can bear to read them, can provide family details, with a few names given in records of arrests and prosecutions as early as the fifteenth century. In Nice, a community of about two hundred Jewish people was permitted to live in the ghetto by the eighteenth century.

France's colonies present a quite different case of the treatment of Jewish people during the *Ancien régime* (e.g. prior to the Revolution). There, those with the Bordeaux patents did not have the same protections and the position of all Jewish people was one of insecurity. They suffered from the same persecution as Protestants after the Revocation of the Edict of Nantes in 1685 brought an end to what slight religious tolerance there had been. To ensure that new and harsher laws of intolerance would be applied in France's colonies as they were in France, specific legislation was written; it became known as the *Code Noir*, the Black Code.

The *Code Noir* banned all non-Catholics from living in the French colonies and ordered that both Jewish people and Protestants who were in the colonies had three months to leave, yet the governors of the colonies did not always apply the law as the king and the Jesuits wished. Though most Protestants were forced to leave the colonies, many Jewish people, so long as they behaved like Christians and did not overtly practice their religion, were allowed by local authorities to remain.

Research

From this briefest of histories can be seen that there are four main difficulties when researching Jewish families in the French records of the *Ancien régime*:

1. The rarity of any records of births, marriages or deaths before the beginning of civil registration in 1792;
2. Almost all Jewish families did not have hereditary surnames, so the genealogical method of searching a previous generation via a surname is not applicable;
3. The rarity of conversions to Christianity means that the many, many parish registers hold little value for this research;
4. The numerous ruptures of the Jewish populations caused by the expulsions mean that there are periods when Jewish people vanished from administrative records.

Nevertheless, there is quite a lot of material, particularly:

- Religious registers, both Catholic and Jewish
- Notarial acts
- Jewish tax lists

It is possible for research into French Jewish families of the *Ancien régime* to be quite successful.

The Catholic Parish Registers

Since 1539, when the law known as the *Ordonnance de Villers-Cotterêts* was passed, it was required for parish priests to record all baptisms, marriages and burials within their parishes. These are the *registres paroissiaux*, or parish registers, covering *baptêmes*, *mariages*, *sépultures* also *inhumations* (burials). These continued to 1792, when they were replaced by civil registrations.

These registers may show those Jewish people who converted. Be aware that, especially in the Jewish communities of Bordeaux and in the colonies, many people publicly converted to Catholicism and privately continued to practice and live by their own religion. Thus, there may be no family record of the conversion but research will show a baptism or marriage of a Jewish person in Catholic parish records.

The necessity of this apparent conversion must not be underestimated. The law considered that only Catholic marriages were legal. Therefore, the children of non-Catholic unions were considered to be illegitimate and, as such, they could not inherit. Thus, a Jewish or Protestant person who married in their own religion but not as Catholics (and to marry as a Catholic, one had to be baptized as a Catholic) could not leave their property and money to their own children; all they possessed went to the King's coffers.

Do read some history of the Jewish communities in an area and see if the research has not already been done. Many Jewish scholars have compiled lists of the entries for certain locations, such as Robert Weyl's listing of baptisms of Jewish people in Strasbourg in the eighteenth century.[3]

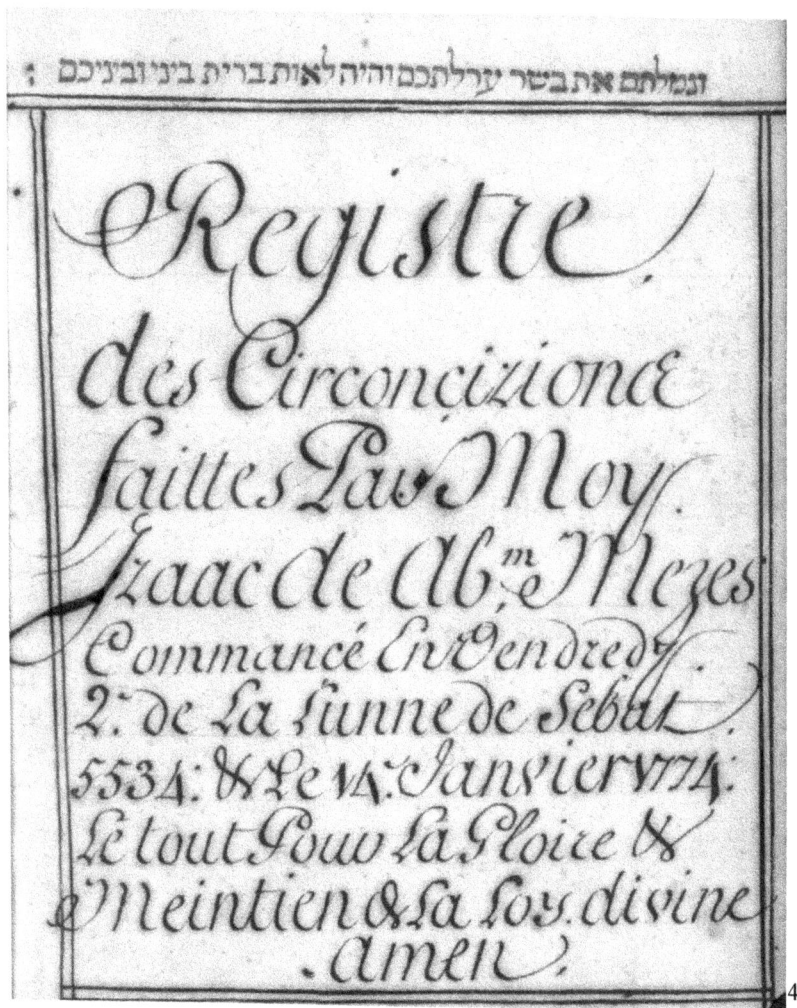

[3] Weyl, Robert. "Baptêmes de Juifs à Strasbourg au XVIIIe siècle », Revue des Etudes juives, tome CXXXVIII (1-2), janvier-juin 1979.

[4] Image source : BORDEAUX GG 848 - Israélites Portugais. - Registre des circoncisions (14 janvier 1774-1er décembre 1793) - 14 janvier 1774-1er décembre 1793. Archives Bordeaux Métropole. https://archives.bordeaux-metropole.fr/

The Jewish Registers

There was no general law like the *Ordonnance de Villers-Cotterêts* that required that Jewish people register their births, marriages and burials. Yet, Jewish registers, written by rabbis, were maintained and some survive. They are a rare and precious resource but there is significant variation from one region to another. Increasingly, they are online, on the websites of Departmental Archives and of Municipal Archives of the larger cities, such as Bordeaux.

1. In the Southwest, some birth, circumcision, marriage and death registers remain for the towns of:
   a. Saint-Esprit
   b. Peyrehorade
   c. Bidache
   d. Bordeaux – found on the website of the Municipal Archives of Bordeaux. (archives.bordeaux.metropole.fr)
   e. The registers of the parish of Saint-Etienne d'Arribe-Labourd at Bayonne - a single microfilm roll which contains a number of Jewish registers, some of them in Spanish, concerning births, circumcisions, marriages and burials. The typed contents list at the beginning of the roll is most helpful. This can be seen on the website of the Departmental Archives of Pyrénées-Atlantiques.

16

2. In the Papal States and Provence, the registers of the ghettos, *les registres des carrières*, are the birth, circumcision, marriage and death registers for:
   a. Avignon
   b. Carpentras
   c. Cavaillon
   d. Isle sur la Sorgue

   Many of these are digitized on the website of the Departmental Archives of Vaucluse.

3. Alsace-Lorraine
   a. In Lorraine's cities, from 1717, Jewish people were required to maintain registers of births, marriages and deaths and some of these have survived.
   b. In Metz and some Alsatian villages, there are a few registers that have survived.

Below is an example of an entry in a Jewish birth register from Saint-Esprit, in the Southwest, for the year 1759.[5] The information that it gives is limited.

---

[5] Saint Esprit (Bayonne), Pyrénées-Atlantiques, Registres paroissiaux et d'état civil, Juifs, Bayonne 1622-1808, Archives départementales des Pyrénées-Atlantiques, http://earchives.le64.fr/

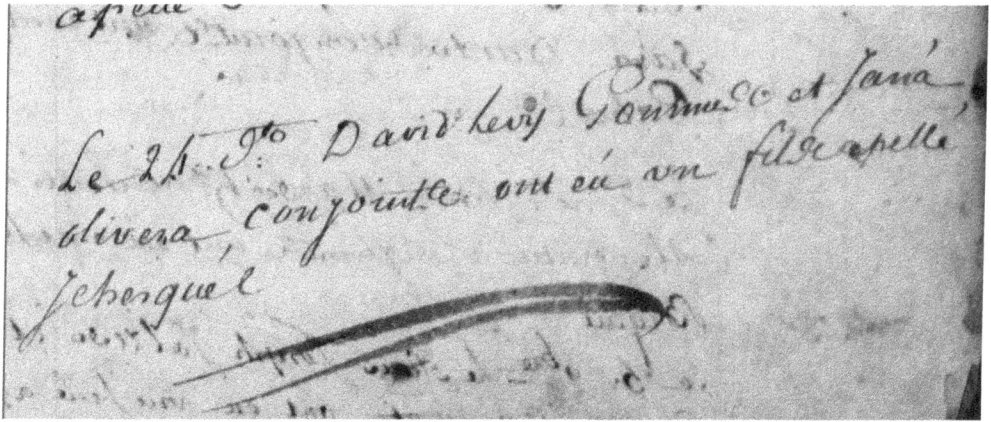

It reads:

> Le 24 9re [1759] David Levy Gommes et Jana [Hana]
> Olivera, conjoints ont eu un fils apellé
> Iehezquél

Translated, this is:

> The 24th of November David Levy Gommes and
> Jana [Hana] Olivera, [who are] married, have had a
> son named Iehezquél

Sadly, the child died some months later, as this death register[6]
entry, in French, shows:

---

[6] Saint Esprit (Bayonne), Pyrénées-Atlantiques, Registres paroissiaux et d'état civil, Juifs,
Bayonne 1622-1808, Archives départementales des Pyrénées-Atlantiques, http://earchives.le64.fr/

It reads:

> Le 10 do deceda Jehezquel fils de David Levy
> Gommes &
> de haná Olivera conjoints

Translated, this is:

> The 10th ditto [February 1762, which was written above]
> died Jehezquel son of David Levy Gommes &
> of haná Olivera, married.

Below is an entry from the circumcision register of Samuel Gomes Atias covering the years 1725-1773 for the town of Bidache and written in Spanish.[7] It gives the child's name, Ysaque Gomes Caseres, the father's name, Daniel, but not the mother's, and the date of the event in 1730 is in both the Hebrew and the Gregorian calendars.

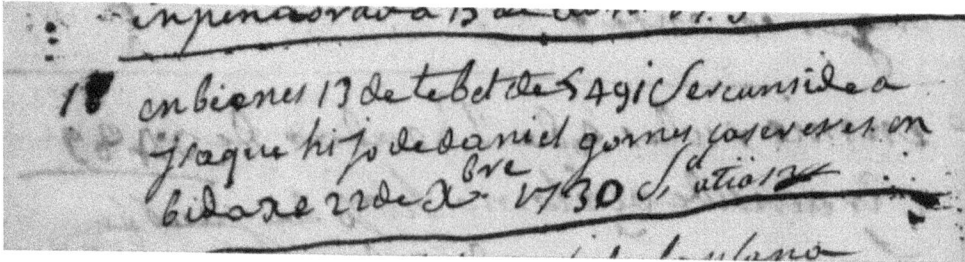

---

[7] Bidache, Pyrénées-Atlantiques, Registres paroissiaux et d'état civil, Bayonne 1622-1808, Archives départementales des Pyrénées-Atlantiques, http://earchives.le64.fr/

Notarial Acts

The *notaire* is a professional with the legal qualifications to draw up all sorts of civil contracts and agreements, called acts, from sales of property to marriage contracts to wills, all of which are legally binding. For centuries, French families have relied on *notaires* and notarial acts to legally protect their decisions. The functions of notaires did not change from the *Ancien régime* through and after the Revolution; only their title changed from *Notaire Royale* to *Notaire de la République*.

Whether the notaires were French or not, the system existed in all three regions where Jewish people lived. In many cases, the same notarial office, known as an *étude*, was used by a family from the *Ancien régime* well into the twentieth century. Increasingly, some original acts and many indices of notarial offices are digitized and found on the websites of the Departmental Archives and, for Paris, the National Archives. The notarial acts most concerned with family affairs and, therefore, of most use to the genealogist are:

- marriage contracts
- death or probate inventories
- wills
- guardianship agreements and accounts

Most of the earlier Jewish marriage contracts, however, were not written by *notaires* but by rabbis but, to ensure their legality, they often were deposited with the *notaire*. This was common in the Southwest, and as was required by law in Alsace.

These Ketubahs, the Jewish religious marriage contracts, detailing the financial maintenance of the bride in the event of death or divorce, are not always easy to find because:

- They usually were given to the family of the bride;
- After the Revolution, the *Consistoires* (see below) usually did not keep a copy;
- If a ketubah were deposited with a *notaire*, to find it you need to know the name of the *notaire*, and there were many, many of them;
- Many for sale online, as they are often quite beautiful and people collect them, so they rarely end up in archives.

An excellent source for those in Alsace, with extracts of over five thousand Jewish marriage contracts of the eighteenth century in the notarial records of Alsace is: *Memoire Juive En Alsace : Contrats de mariage au XVIIIe siècle* by André Aaron Fraenkel.

[8] Ketubah image: Nice, France, 1690, February 17. Beinecke Rare Book and Manuscript Library. Yale University Library. https://collections.library.yale.edu/catalog/2020715?child_oid=1082877

The Jewish Census or Tax Records

These lists were compiled in order to monitor the Jewish communities for tax purposes. They can be found in all three of the regions discussed. They usually name only the heads of the families and do not list each person in the family. They can be found primarily in the Departmental Archives but some are in the National Archives.

One of the most important is the 1784 census of Jewish people in Alsace. The index to it can be searched on the website of GenAmi (of which more, below).[9]

---

[9] www.genami.org

Aids in *Ancien régime* Jewish Research

- *Les Familles juives en France, XVIe siècle – 1815, guide des recherches biographiques et généalogiques* by Gildas Bernard, published by the *Archives nationales* in 1990.

To know the holdings related to Jewish people up to 1815 in the public archives of France, there is no better source than Bernard's book. It contains detailed essays written by local, expert archivists on each region. He gives complete lists, for every Departmental Archive, of all archival series that concern or even mention Jewish people. In a separate section, he also includes anything in the *Archives nationales* (National Archives), the *Bibliothèque nationale* (National Library) as well as in smaller facilities. The archival codes also are given, though these may have changed. The book is in many libraries and genealogy collections but, unfortunately, at the time of writing, it is not online.

- The website of GenAmi : www.genami.org

The Jewish Genealogy Association maintains a website with huge amounts of information on French and European Jewish genealogy of all time periods. For each region, they have written excellent Research Guides, providing advice and links. The guides are free to read, but one must pay a fee to join the Association and be able to access the rest of the material.

- Departmental Archives websites

Some of the *Archives départementales* (Departmental Archives) have written their own Research Guides about

French Jewish genealogy, specific to their own collections, with clear instructions on how to use them. That of the department of Bas-Rhin is one of the best. Most are being written all the time so keep checking the aids to research on those websites. They are free and can be downloaded.

- *Inventaire-Sommaire des Archives Départementales antérieure à 1790*

Archives guides with the title above, describing the pre-Revolutionary, *Ancien régime* holdings, were written for each of the Departmental Archives and all are online. Many are on Google Books. Essentially archival finding aids, they give extremely detailed listings and descriptions, by archival code, of all of the collections, not only those records relating to Jewish people.

To find them, type the title above into your search engine, in quotation marks, then add the name of the department you want. When you find the scanned book, use the search or find function to search for any of the following words:
  o juif
  o juifs
  o juive
  o juives
  o israélite
  o or a name you are seeking

The French Revolution, the First Empire and Jewish Liberties

The French Revolution was as monumental for French Jewish people as for all others in France. In 1789, there were approximately forty thousand Jewish people in what would become France, still, for the most part, in separate groups: Sephardim in the Southwest, Avignan and Comtat Venaissin, Ashkenazim in Alsace and Lorraine, and mixed Jewish people in Paris.

The Revolution brought significant new rights for Jewish people. In 1790 full citizenship was granted to the Jewish people in the Southwest. After two years of debate, full French citizenship was granted to all Jewish people in the country in 1791. This emancipation of Jewish people in France made all previous laws concerning them obsolete, including the patents. So, it was not entirely positive for all of the Jewish communities.

Napoleon came to power in 1799 and was crowned Emperor in 1804. There followed a rapid series of events important to French Jewish people:

- In 1804, the *Code Civil* was established, providing written laws for all aspects of civil life for all citizens of France.
- In 1806, the Jewish religion was officially recognized. An *Assemblée des notables*, or Grand Sanhédrin, was convened to propose how to integrate Jewish customs with the *Code Civil* and new French civil society. To further this liaison between French civil law and Jewish custom, the Central *Consistoire* was created in Paris.
- In 1807, the Grand Sanhédrin submitted its proposals
- In 1808, Napoleon mandated the choosing of hereditary surnames (see below) and regional *consistoires* were

created to ensure Jewish compliance with the Code Civil.
They were in:

- Paris*
- Strasbourg*
- Wintzenheim
- Mayence*
- Metz*
- Nancy*
- Trèves
- Coblentz
- Crefeld
- Bordeaux*
- Marseilles*
- Turin
- Casal

At the fall of the Empire and the loss of Italian and Prussian territories, only those with asterisks following their names remained, but the records of the others survive in many cases. There are now fifteen *consistoires* and they serve as the centres of their Jewish communities.

Pick a Name - *Le Décret de Bayonne*

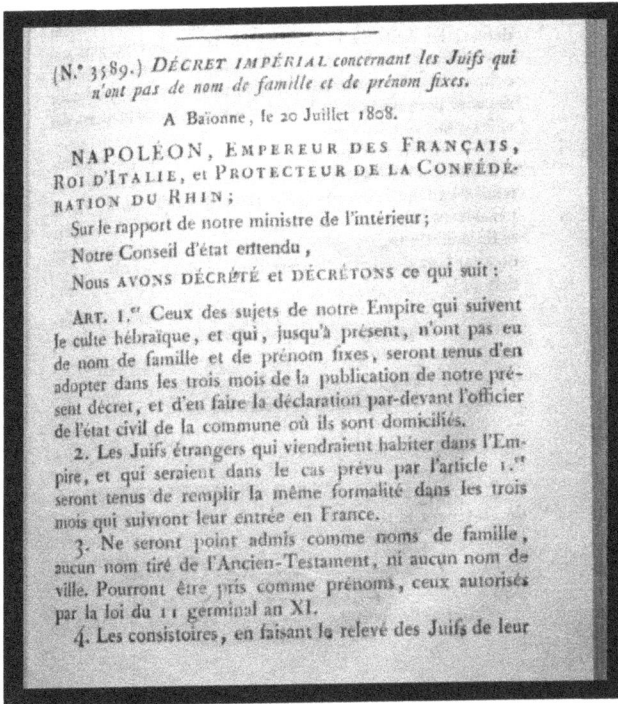

With the *Décret de Bayonne*, issued on the 20th of July, 1808, Napoleon ordered that all Jewish people in France (or who were immigrating permanently to France) who did not have a fixed and hereditary surname be required to choose one.

They had to go to the town hall and declare their names to the mayor, who entered them into a register book. These Registers of Jewish Name Choices (*registres d'options de noms 1808*) became a de facto census of the Jewish people of France (to be followed in some places by a real census a year later).

The numbers are interesting. According to a list in the *Archives nationales* (code F19 11010) there were 46,054 Jewish people in France who chose permanent names. The majority were in the departments of Bas-Rhin, Haut-Rhin (with some nicely legible examples for the city of Mulhouse), and Moselle. In each, the head of a family, usually the husband and father, gives for each family member his or her name, date and place of birth, and the surname and forenames chosen. The registrations have the appearance and structure of any other civil register entry, *acte d'état civil,* in 1808.

The originals are in the Communal or the Departmental Archives of the region where they were first recorded, in Series E. Summaries and reports on these options are in the *Archives nationales.* As with any such documentation, not all have survived. Those in Strasbourg were burned in the bombing during the Franco-Prussian War, for example, and those of Moselle were destroyed during the Second World War.

Many of the websites of Departmental Archives have digitized the registers of declarations of hereditary surnames, as did that of Bas-Rhin. The registers give the names and usually the ages of a couple and all of their children adopting the new name.

The excellent *Cercle de Généalogie Juive* (of which more below) offers for sale from their (bilingual!) site volumes by the late Pierre Katz, an expert on Alsatian Jewry, of extracts of the data from the *registres d'options de noms* for the departments of Bas-Rhin, Haut-Rhin, Moselle, and Meurthe-et-Moselle. Most helpfully, they also have an alphabetical list on the website of all the surnames for Bas-Rhin, showing the villages where they were declared.

According to many, *the registres d'options de noms 1808* are where French Jewish genealogy begins.

Should you have the chance to visit the Departmental Archives in person, you could stumble across a great deal more from this period. Each department did something slightly different. For example, in the city of Brest in the department of Finistère, the authorities, when making a list of Jewish people with their new names, also listed other information. Below is a list of Jewish men married to Catholic women that states whether or not their children were baptized as Catholics.

As can be seen, some very useful genealogical information is provided:

10 *Culte Israélite*, 3V13, Archives départementales de Finistère

- The men's names
- Their ages
- Their professions
- Their places of birth (all of them came from Alsace-Lorraine)
- How long they had lived in Brest
- That their unnamed wives were Catholic
- How many children they had
- Who had been baptized

As is so often the case, the above was held in an archive series concerned with anyone non-Catholic. The series is entitled "*cultes*", e.g. non-Catholics, and covers:

- Protestants, their church accounts, how they were policed, their temple, and how they were counted in a census;
- Jewish people or *Israélites*, the 1808 name choices and censuses, taxes, issues of anti-Semitism;
- The "New" Catholic Church

Links:

Cercle de Généalogie Juive

https://www.genealoj.org/fr

Changing Names to Assimilate...and Back Again

As individuals within a species, we are all pretty much identical; no one would mistake any of us for an elephant or a spider or a barracuda. Yet, how we focus on the differences of our fellow humans, blinding ourselves to the similarities and thus, to the possibility of unity. Dividing ourselves into groups based upon minute differences, our larger and dominant groups make life hell for the smaller groups, who in turn, make life hell for groups smaller than they. One would laugh, if only not to weep.

French Jewish people, in an effort to assimilate, have often changed their surnames to sound more French. After the Second World War, government officials, at the local level most often, urged Jewish residents and immigrants to change their surnames. About five per cent did so. Many of their descendants now wish to change their names back to those of their grandfathers, even though they are sympathetic to those who made the changes. As one descendant said of his grandfather to a *Los Angeles Times* reporter: "He never complained [about being encouraged to change his name]. Remember these were people who, after what they had been through, just wanted to live in peace. They would do anything to blend in."[11]

At the time of the changes, some were told that their children could, on reaching the age of majority, choose to take back the family's previous surname. This was simply not true. One must apply for a court order -- something not lightly given in France -- and have a very good reason to change one's name. Some people felt that their "Frenchified" names make them feel cut off from their roots. In April, 2013, the courts at last granted French

11 Kim Wilsher. "Some Jews in France wish to revert to family names", *Los Angeles Times*, 17 July 2010.

Jewish people the right to change their names back to earlier names used by the families.

One such descendant, the psychoanalyst Cécile Masson, has formed an organization for those who wish to take back their family's earlier names, *La Force du Nom*. A discussion of the issues with her and others can be heard on the internet radio site of France Culture on the presentation entitled "*Du changement de nom au re-nom*". Ms. Masson has produced a documentary on the subject, of an hour and a bit, based on interviews with some Jewish families of Ashkenazi origin.

Should your research into Jewish ancestry in France have run aground, a name change may be why.

Links:

La Force du Nom:

http://laforcedunom.free.fr/la_force_du_nom/accueil.html

Listen to : "*Du changement de nom au re-nom*" :

https://www.radiofrance.fr/franceculture/podcasts/la-fabrique-de-l-histoire/du-changement-de-nom-au-re-nom-rediffusion-de-l-emission-du-27-09-11-2193020

The Archives of the *Consistoire de Paris*

In researching Jewish families of Paris, the *Consistoire de Paris* provides a unique resource. Before going, one should have all possible civil register entries (*actes d'état civil*) and other documentation about births, marriages and deaths. This will greatly aid in using the archives of the *Consistoire*. The holdings include:

- Register books of marriages in Paris synagogues tied to the *Consistoire* from 1822 onwards; these will give the name of the Rabbi officiating, at which synagogue the marriage took place and, often, whether it was a charity wedding;
- Register books of burials, from 1882 onwards; in addition to the name of the deceased, the age, address, and hour of burial, these give, most importantly, the name of the cemetery, allowing one to then go to find the grave;
- Names from the lists of various censuses of Jewish people in Paris
- A number of publications which have extracted information from the above censuses and register books, in particular, the book entitled "*Relevé des Ketoubot au Consistoire de Paris, 1872-1884*" by Veronique Cahen.

The *Consistoire* is located in the 9th arrondissement in a building with high security. To use the archives, one must telephone first and make an appointment. On arrival, one is escorted to the reading room, where there are no archives, but the shelves contain 100 years of *L'Univers Isréalite* and of *Archives Isréalites*. One must explain what is being researched and the appropriate volumes will be fetched from the nether regions and brought forth. The gentleman who does the fetching will also suggest other research possibilities. Photographs of the registers are permitted; photocopying is not. We had a very successful research day, finding the cemeteries where a number of the people we have been researching are buried. Afterward, we visited the cemeteries and took many photos of the graves that still exist.

Outside of Paris, one of best websites for digitized *consistoire* records of the Alsace-Lorraine region is the Center for Jewish History. They write that they have filmed records of 139 Jewish communities in Alsace and Lorraine, predominantly from the nineteenth century: "Records of the Consistoire Central des Israélites de France, as well as of the local consistories for the departments of Bas-Rhin and Haut-Rhin (Alsace) and Moselle and Meurthe-et-Moselle (Lorraine), in Strasbourg, Colmar, Metz and Nancy, including minutes, tax-lists, lists of rabbis, cantors, and notables, censuses of Jewish communities, and correspondence."

Links:

Archives du Consistoire de Paris

www.consistoire.org

Center for Jewish History

www.cjh.org

L'Univers Isréalite is on the Internet Archive:

https://archive.org/details/luniversisralit01unkngoog/page/n9/mode/1up?view=theater

Certificates of Good Character from *Consistoires*

The network of consistories in France, which serve as the liaison between Jewish law and French law, was created in 1808. The *Consistoire Central* is at the head of the network and is based in Paris. Their archives are described above. Their holdings that one may be permitted to see are often limited to very basic registers, which give less information than can be found in French civil registers. (The one exception being that the *Consistoire* death registers can give the place of burial, which civil registers do not give.)

So, we were quite delighted to come across a small collection of letters emanating from the Paris Consistory in 1808. They were letters of good character, much like the *certificats de bonne vie et moeurs* requested from a mayor about recently arrived Jewish residents of his city. The requests clearly followed the requirement that the mayors record the mandated selection of hereditary surnames by Jewish people, explained above. These character references were not required by law and so one would not expect to find them in every municipal or departmental archive but we now think that, having found them once, we will look for them on every visit.

These were found in the Departmental Archives of Finistère and were gathered by the city of Brest. They had been placed in the series 3V - "*Cultes*", which meant any religion that was not Catholic, and relate to the Jewish, Protestant and "New Catholic" communities.

Translated, the example above reads:

> As concerns the certificate delivered by the Municipal Council of the city of Brest on the 23rd of June 1810 to Mr. Isaac Norden, domiciled at Brest in the Department of Finistère, which states that the said Isaac Norden has not engaged in illicit traffic or trade in any way, after having gathered information concerning the morality of this gentleman, I can attest, conforming with article 7 of the Imperial Decree of March 1808, his good conduct and probity. In witness whereof I have delivered to him the present certificate to be used for all legal intents and purposes.
>
> Done in the Consistory of Paris on 16 July 1810"

As records relating to individual Jewish people of this period are often hard to find, we consider this a bit of a treasure.

Cimetière parisien de Pantin - **The Pantin Cemetery**

Someone asked us to investigate the Pantin Cemetery. We dragged our weary self out to nearly the end of Line Seven on the Métro and hiked a long, traffic-blasted and gusty avenue to the entry. It looks rather battered but elegant in online photos.

What one truly sees on approaching the entry is four or five disembowelled sofas, rubbish bins, and a wide selection of empty beer bottles making for a different sort of depression from that usual to cemetery visits. Cross the threshold, however, and one is transported from grim poverty to grand avenues of beautiful gardens and mature trees. There are more than eight thousand trees, and the air is correspondingly cleaner than out on the road. A very nice place to spend eternity.

The Pantin cemetery is outside of the city of Paris, on the border between Pantin and Bobigny. Administratively, however, it is one of the Paris cemeteries. It is the largest cemetery in France and in Europe. It opened on the 15th of November, 1886, and has over 200,000 graves in 180 divisions, of which many are designated as Jewish divisions.

Graves and tombs in France are considered inviolable, except as concerns the bureaucrats, who can do as they please with the dead as well as with the living. The space in cemeteries could once have been bought as *concessions à perpétuité*, e.g., forever. Descendants merely had to keep up the tombs (they have a tendency to cave in if not maintained, and can be quite dangerous). And there's the rub. The population explosion having affected the cemeteries along with everything else involving humanity, the problem of overcrowded cemeteries has become urgent. In 2002, it was announced that all of the Paris cemeteries were full; there was absolutely no place for anyone to be buried. The press was full of comic headlines saying such things as "Death in Paris is Forbidden". The solution has been to review the maintenance and condition of all of the graves taken as *concessions à perpétuité,* (and there are reportedly some 1,157,533 in Paris,) and reclaim those that have clearly been forgotten. There are rules:

- the grave has to have been abandoned for a minimum of thirty years
- there must be an effort to find the family lasting at least four years
- there must be a public notice that the grave is planned to be reclaimed unless family come forward
- if the family do come forward, they have up to three years to make repairs; if they fail to do so, the bones will be exhumed and sent to the ossuary (in Père Lachaise Cemetery)

As repairs can cost up to 10,000 euros, one can be sympathetic to the families that have let the graves fall into disrepair. Nevertheless, there is a waiting list of dead, we read, though we cannot work out just where they are waiting, and the pressure on the cemetery administrators is intense. Many Jewish families want plots in the Jewish sections, many Muslim families want plots facing Mecca, many Christian families want plots in the Christian sections. Everyone wants plots near to relatives. Consequently, efforts to reclaim space have increased significantly.

Pantin is run as are the other cemeteries. The summer and winter hours correspond to the hours of daylight. To find a grave, you must have the full name of the deceased and the date of burial or at least that of death. With that information, you can go to the office, which is just at the entry, and request directions to the grave. The guards wait outside and in a most kind and un-Parisian way will offer to drive you to the correct section, if you feel it may be too far to walk. The cemetery is so large that cars are permitted, should you wish to take one.

If you think that your ancestor may be at Pantin, and you wish to plunk the small fortune to protect his or her grave for a bit longer, you can write to the administration:

Cimetière parisien de Pantin
164, avenue Jean-Jaurès
93 Pantin

Considering cemeteries generally, in addition to the work done by GenAmi and the *Cercle de Généalogie juive*, there are some websites of help.

- Find a Grave (www.findagrave.com) now has all of the names from the Shoah Memorial (see below), one Jewish cemetery and a Paris cemetery that has a large Jewish section. It is not the best source.
- There is a similar project on Geneanet (www.geneanet.org) which is much better, but still limited.
    o It has very good photographs, which can show if a Star of David is on the stone
    o The database can be searched by keyword, which allows one to enter *juif* or *juive*

From 1792 - Modern Civil Registers

Civil registration of births, marriages and deaths became law in 1792, even before the Code Civil of 1804. Civil registration is:

- Required by law for everyone, regardless of religion
- Replaces legally all religious birth or baptism, marriage, burial registrations. From this point forward only a civil registration of a birth can prove legitimacy or parentage, only a civil registration of a marriage is proof of marriage and only a civil registration of a death is proof of death.
- The precise format for writing a registration is given in the Code Civil. Nothing may be altered or added. For example, French death register entries do not give the cause of death. Early registers, especially those from 1792 to 1804 have quite irregular wording at times.
- Civil registration must take place BEFORE a religious ceremony. Thus, if you are seeking the record of a religious marriage, you would look for a date AFTER the civil marriage took place.

There are three categories of civil registration and they are to be found in three registers (though small towns used to put them all in a single book).

- A register of birth registrations, *actes de naissance*, including recognitions, transcriptions of relative court orders, and affidavits concerning the newborn.

- A register of marriages, *actes de mariage*, including transcriptions of divorces and annulments, transcriptions of relative court orders, and affidavits concerning the marriage, and the marriage banns.

- A register of deaths, *actes de décès*, including actes of stillbirths, and transcriptions of relative court orders and affidavits concerning the death.

ACCESS to these records by the public is now:

- 75 years after the closure of the register for birth and marriage register entries
- Immediately after the closure of the register for death register entries.

Most civil registers through 1902 have been microfilmed and are freely available on the websites of the Departmental Archives. Many but not all are available via a number of different commercial genealogy websites. For years after 1902, continued digitizing really depends upon the budget of the specific Departmental Archives. Some, such as those of Paris, have civil registers through the 1930s digitized, while others have nothing after 1902 and little hope of anything more being available online any time soon.

Naturalizations

It may seem odd, but some people chose to become French and when they did so, the process was termed *naturalisation*. One completed an application that was a *demande de naturalisation*, added much identifying and supporting documentation, and sent it off to the authorities. They would approve or disapprove the application and, if they did approve, send a certificate.

The benefits of naturalization usually had to do with one's children, especially if a father were the one becoming French as, for most of the nineteenth century, children born in France had the same nationality as their father. If he became French, they could inherit and have certain other advantages permitted nationals alone, such as serving in the army. Conversely, if he remained foreign, he might inherit from his non-French family, and his children were exempt from French conscription. One can imagine various scenarios where one choice or the other would be more advantageous to a family.

The National Archives of France, les *Archives nationales*, have a jumbo-sized collection of the application files, or dossiers. The site in Pierrefitte-sur-Seine has those dating from about 1789 to 1948. The information in a file can range from just about nothing to:

- the full name
- place of birth
- date of birth
- address in France
- family members
- a copy the birth registrations, with translation, of the applicant, spouse and children
- proofs as to financial solvency
- documentation of service in another nation's military, if applicable
- proof of employment
- a letter from the town hall confirming place and length of residency
- a letter from the prefecture supporting the application
- a letter from the police confirming that the applicant had no criminal record

Quite a nice snapshot of a person and a family!

These files are absolutely crucial to any research on nineteenth century Jewish families in France and on the families of the refugees from the German annexation of Alsace-Lorraine. The former were often immigrants from other parts of Europe, while the latter, if they did not claim French nationality, would have had to apply to be "reintegrated".

The Naturalization Files, *dossiers de naturalisation,* are in the process of being put online, and many of them are already available on the website of the *Archives nationales*.

For the years 1855 to 1918, one can search the *Bulletin de lois*. This will show only the successful applicants. From 1948 onward, the case will have been mentioned in the *Journal Officiel* or will be in an alphabetical listing held at the archives.

In this way, some families that arrived in France from elsewhere can, if they chose to stay, be traced with some rather thrilling success.

Links:

The Naturalization Files digitized on the *Archives nationales* website:

https://www.siv.archives-nationales.culture.gouv.fr/siv/cms/content/helpGuide.action?uuid=804c95a9-6550-4b00-b97b-78b0d52816cd&version=6&preview=false&typeSearch=&searchString

Alternatively, you can try typing in the person's name in the search form on the *Archives nationales* website:

https://www.siv.archives-nationales.culture.gouv.fr/siv/rechercheconsultation/recherche/ir/rechercheGeneraliste.action

The French Police Surveillance Dossiers of the Interwar Period - *les Fonds de Moscou* - Have an Index Online

Very exciting news on the indexing front. For a vast collection of the dossiers of some 650,000 people on whom the French security police were spying, for the most part between the two World Wars, there is now online an index to all of the names contained therein. The index was created in Russian, for this collection has travelled more than many of us ever will.

During the occupation of Paris in World War Two, the Nazis collected a great many things, including artworks, books and archives, and sent them to Germany. Among the archives taken were the private papers of the French branch of the Rothschild family, the library and archives of the *Alliance Isréalite Universelle*, the Masonic archives and membership records of the *Grand Orient de France* and the police surveillance files of the Directorate for National Security in the Ministry of the Interior.

All of these collections now are called the "*Fonds de Moscou*", the "Moscow Collection". This is because one of the conquerors of the Nazis was the Soviet Union and, dutifully following the claim by a nineteenth century American Secretary of War that "to the victor belong the spoils", the Red Army stole from the Nazis what they had stolen from the French and took it all to Moscow, where (words not being minced) they were known as the "Trophy Archives". No one conquered the Soviet Union but itself; when it collapsed, word got out that archival treasures that France had thought lost forever were not so. It took some "discussion", but this is something at which the French are unparalleled, so the Russians bowed and the collections were returned, or mostly so.

The surveillance files part of the *Fonds de Moscou* are in the *Archives nationales* at Pierrefitte-sur-Seine and a full research guide has been published on the website. The English version can be downloaded:

https://www.siv.archives-
nationales.culture.gouv.fr/mm/media/download/FRAN_ANX_013482.pdf

The files cover the types the police found suspect and worthy of surveillance:

- Anarchists
- Anti-military or war agitators
- Communists
- Political militants
- Foreign residents requesting an identity card
- Foreign spies or those suspected of aiding foreign intelligence organizations
- Foreigners who had been in prison or expelled from their countries
- Gamblers banned from casinos and those authorised to work in casinos
- Foreigners whose requests to remain had been denied and who were expelled
- Foreigners who requested to be naturalized
- French who requested passports to travel and foreigners who requested permission to remain in France
- Jewish people

Quelle liste!

The website warns that using the index is not easy.

In essence, the first index is a partially alphabetical (through the first three letters only) listing of names, mostly but not all of them French, made by Soviet archivists in Russian, in notebooks that have been microfilmed and those images digitized.

1. This was made by archivists to be a simple name index to the named files or dossiers.
2. The index of names refers to a dossier's number.
3. There are numerous linguistic issues that require that a search for a name be tried many times in many ways:
    1. Articles are treated as the first letter of a name. All names beginning with "de" will be under D. All those beginning with "le" or "la" will be under L.
    2. All those beginning with "van" or "von" will be under V or W (see below). This presents real problems when one recalls that the names are in alphabetical order only through the third letter.
    3. "Mac" is usually seen as a middle name. Thus William MacCabe is under "Cabe, William Mac"
    4. No spaces between components of names were permitted. Thus "Le Blanc" will be treated as "Leblanc" (actually a help under the third letter limit.)
    5. The original dossiers, created by the French bureaucrats, may but not necessarily will have foreign names altered to be more French. Thus, "Karl" might have been altered to "Charles". (Clearly, the bureaucrats were not trained as genealogists.)
    6. The Cyrillic alphabet of the indexers did not accommodate the names written by the creators. Thus, V and W are often confused; Q and X come after Z.
4. Some files were missed out in the indexing so, there being no way to insert them, there is a supplementary index that also must be searched.

There is also a microfilmed and digitized card index, made by the Directorate of General Security, in French, of all of the two million names mentioned in the dossiers.

1. This was made by the original creators for their own use in surveillance and covers all of the types of files.
2. The cards do not always refer to a file or dossier.
3. Some cards may refer to dossiers that were not taken to Moscow but are in the Archives nationales, such as
    a. Foreigners who were expelled between 1889 and 1906, which are in the Police series of F/7
4. Some files were closed and destroyed but the card might remain, with the word "*détruit*" written on it.
5. The cards contain some biographical information and, in a few cases, photographs.

Searching the Indices and Finding the Code In Order to Request a Dossier

In order to request a dossier, one needs:

1. The number of the archival series. This is a random accession number, as is the way with archives. They all begin with 1994, followed by more numbers, then by a slash.
2. The number of the carton comes after the slash
3. The number of the file "dossier no. x"
4. The name on the file

Numbers 1 through 3 can be found by entering the name, surname first, in the main "Advanced search" form of the *Salle des Inventaires Virtuelle* page of the website.

Scrolling through the images of the indices in order to find the codes is fraught with innumerable, irritating flaws. For example, one can click to see the filmed images for one code, then scroll onto those of the following code without realizing it, which the automatically presented code does not change, though now wrong, and the handwritten code at the top of the page is indecipherable.

Considering all that these archives suffered (let alone what was suffered by the poor souls who were its subjects) and all of the various indignities of shuffled provenance, perhaps we should accept the irritations and be grateful that they have survived, are available, and can be accessed at all.

Once again, we genealogists really must thank the archivists at the *Archives nationales*. Keep checking their English page, cited above, for updates as they improve the access.

Marrying in Wartime France

We have received a query by e-mail from *Madame* Y, the response to which we think might be of interest to all. "What documentation was necessary to marry during the war in France?"

This has entailed a bit of research and we are not fully confident to have found the most complete information for a reply. Nevertheless, we shall share what we have been able to find.

Firstly, World War Two is referred to in French as "La Guerre 1939 à 1945". And that is broken into parts: 1939-1940 (when France was at war with Nazi Germany), a sort of "Period About Which One Does Not Speak" (the Occupation and Vichy), and 1944-1945 (Liberation).

Secondly, there were two Frances: the northern part, under Nazi occupation, and the southern part under the Vichy Régime. As far as we have been able to determine, the *Code Civil* (France's Civil Code, which legislates many aspects of civil life, first published in 1804 and still in effect, with modernization, of course, today) continued to be in effect in both parts for the entirety of the war.

- The age of majority was twenty-one; a man and a woman who both had reached that age could marry without their parents' permission.
- Civil marriage had to take place before religious marriage.
- From 1907, women had had the right to keep their salaries
- From 1838, they no longer were required to obey their husbands

The Vichy Régime was openly xenophobic, excessively patriarchal and rather maniacally puritanical. Some of the Vichy laws and regulations included:

- Prohibiting divorce for the first three years of marriage, and making it more difficult in any case (from 2 April 1941)
- Many efforts to increase the birth rate, including adjusting the salaries of civil servants based upon the number of children they had; prohibiting the recruitment of married women to the civil service, increasing allowances to families, continuing to allow anonymous births, offering a dowry to working women who would quit and marry, etc.
- Many laws against alcoholic drinks
- What one author termed a "merciless war on abortion"
- The repression of homosexuality
- Severe punishment of adultery
- The requirement of a health certificate before marriage, the *certificat prénuptial*, (from 16 December 1942)

The Vichy government also urged all authorities to apply the laws most rigidly to "foreigners, naturalized or not, communists, and Jewish people". It was not illegal for foreigners to marry but every step of the way would have been made very difficult, e.g., it might have been hard to find a doctor who would give the health certificate, one's naturalization papers would have been demanded, queried, more documents required, etc.

Every effort was made to enforce a patriarchal family structure and to remove women from professional and working life. These same restrictions (but not the allowances or dowries) were applied to men over the age of fifty and to all foreigners.

To learn more:

- Lots of statistics on wartime marriages: *"Guerre et nuptialité. Rélexions sur l'influence de la seconde Guerre mondiale, et de deux autres, sur la nuptialité des Français"* by Francis Ronsin in *Population*, 1995, vol.550, no.1, pp.119-148.
- Superb study of what life was like for women in Vichy France : *"Les Femmes pendant la Seconde Guerre mondiale : un regard porté sur les Étampoises"*, by Joëlle Surply.

  https://www.mairie-etampes.fr/wp-content/uploads/2022/08/MEMOIRES-ETAMPES_24_FEMMES-2e-GM.pdf
- Equally superb chronology of women's rights in France: *"Chronologie des Droits des Femmes en France de La Révolution Française à Nos Jours"* by Hélène Duffuler-Vialle, on the most informative website, Criminocorpus.

  https://criminocorpus.org/fr/legislation/chronologies/chronologie-des-droits-des-femmes-en-france-de-la-revolution-fra/

Œuvre de Secours aux Enfants

The *Œuvre de Secours aux Enfants*, (literally, Work in the Aid of Children, but also known in English as the Society for Rescuing Children), is not originally a French organisation. It was formed in Saint Petersburg in 1912 to help Jewish children whose health had suffered because of persecution. The organisation itself was persecuted and moved first to Berlin, then to France, just before the Second World War.

With the German occupation and the beginning of killings and deportations, OSE expanded its efforts to save children, including two hundred German Jewish children who arrived between March and May, 1939. As the situation became more desperate, every effort was made to try to equip the children with the skills to survive. Many were also given new names and placed with families. There is a quite powerful documentary about one of the OSE orphanages, "The Children of Chabannes", which tells the story.

We visited the headquarters of the OSE in Paris to speak to the archivist for a woman who was rescued as a child, and who now lives in North America. She wanted to trace her brothers, if possible. She had tried searching the records at the *Mémorial de la Shoah* (see below) but, because her brothers were not deported, their names were not in that database. She did not know if they may not have been deported under different names -- perhaps those given by OSE -- or if they had survived. The archivist was able to find their records.

To find someone in the OSE records, write to the Archivist, giving as much information as possible:

- The child's birth name
- Date of birth
- Parents' names
- Siblings names
- An address
- Which orphanage the child was in

It is understood that it may not be possible to provide all of this information and the archivist encourages the inclusion of any memories about people or places, for this may help identify the orphanage. As their goal is to reunite families, there is a certain flexibility in allowing relatives to have access to the records.

The OSE continues as a very active charity providing help to many: the elderly, the handicapped, the homeless. It is possible to make a donation on their website. Click on "*Dons*".

Links:

OSE:
https://www.ose-france.org/

See "The Children of Chabannes":
https://childrenofchabannes.org/

Documents on the Jewish Community
of 18th Century Paris

DOCUMENTS

SUR

LES JUIFS A PARIS

AU XVIIIe SIÈCLE

ACTES D'INHUMATION ET SCELLÉS.

INTRODUCTION.

Au XVIIIe siècle, comme on sait, l'état civil de chaque sujet coïncide avec son état religieux. C'est le curé qui continue à tenir registre, et ce qu'il inscrit c'est non pas tant la naissance, le mariage ou le décès des individus que le baptême, l'union religieuse ou la sépulture. Sans doute l'ordonnance de 1667 [1] et la déclaration de 1736 [2] « laïcisent » ce qu'on appelle alors l'état des hommes et organisent de façon plus efficace le contrôle de l'État [3]. Mais l'état civil n'existe toujours, pourrait-on dire, qu'en fonction de l'état religieux.

Quelle est, dans ces conditions, la situation des non-catho-

---

1. Titre XX, art. 7, sqq. dans Isambert, *Recueil général des anciennes lois françaises*, XVIII, p. 137.

2. Isambert, XXI, p. 405.

3. Le curé est obligé de tenir deux registres, dont l'un est ensuite déposé au greffe du juge royal, et il est loisible d'en demander un extrait soit au curé, soit à l'agent civil. Sur la résistance du clergé à l'application de l'édit de 1736, voy. L. Cahen, *La Question de l'état civil à Paris au XVIIIe siècle*, dans la *Révolution française*, t. LVII (1909), p. 193.

1

60

In 1913, the Society of the History of Paris and of the Ile de France brought out a book by Paul Hildenfinger, *Documents sur les Juifs à Paris au XVIIIe Siècle : Actes d'Inhumation et Scellés*. This is doubly a treasure, since pre-1871 Paris genealogy and pre-Revolutionary French Jewish genealogy are both very difficult areas of research.

The author, who spent months researching the documentation of the deaths of Jewish people in Paris in the eighteenth century, did not live to see the publication. Originally from Lille, he trained at the *Ecole des Chartes* as an archivist and paleographer, then worked at the *Bibliothèque Nationale*. The research for this book did not come from his work but from his personal interest.

As Hildenfinger explains in his Introduction, eighteenth century French law stated that priests or curates were required to maintain registers of births, marriages and burials of every member of their parish. The law did not extend to non-Catholics, who were refused burial in Catholic cemeteries. While many Protestant pastors kept near-identical registers, the leaders of other religions often did not, or those records have not survived. However, it was also required by law that the police were not to allow any burial without some sort of record of death. This particular law, enacted in 1736, was primarily intended for the documentation of Protestants and stated that, where there was no Catholic parish record of burial, an affidavit concerning the deceased was required before burial could take place. It ended up being applied to those of other religions, including Greek Orthodox and Jewish, as well as to a variety of foreigners, duellists and suicides.

It was the local police superintendent, of whom there were about twenty in Paris, who went to the home of the deceased and wrote the necessary documentation. Those documents that remain are in the Y series of the *Archives nationales* and it is these that Mr. Hildenfinger abstracted. Generally, he tells, the documentation includes:

1. The declaration of death, by witnesses, neighbours or friends, whether Christian or Jewish, with their full names, the places of origin, their addresses in Paris. Sometime there may also be their professions and their relationship to the deceased. They signed, in French or Hebrew.
2. The death report and identification of the corpse, with the full name, age, address, religion, and place of origin of the deceased.
3. After 1737, comments by the Attorney General of Châtelet, to whom the report had to be submitted, giving the name of the deceased and the place of burial.
4. The police authorisation for burial.

The *scellé* refers to the documentation concerning the sealing off by law of the deceased's property in order to protect the heirs and/or creditors. Often, it was used by the state to take possession of the property.

In all, Hildenfinger found 176 documents about 171 Jewish persons who died and describes them fully. The index is excellent. The Introduction could be used as a research guide to the subject on its own.

Read it on Gallica at this link:
https://gallica.bnf.fr/ark:/12148/bpt6k6481515v/f19.image

La Revue des Etudes Juives

You know how it is when the research bug bites and it is impossible to stop. More, when the discoveries come thick and fast, you think you have struck some sort of gold, as indeed it can be -- a lovely, golden flow of discovery of history and ideas and family connection. In short, we have found a gem we wish to share about French Jewish genealogical research: *La Revue des études juives*, begun in Paris by the *Société des Etudes Juives* in 1880 and still going strong. Long articles, scholarly and erudite -- especially in the earlier volumes -- provide abundant information that is not only historical but often genealogical. We give examples of titles:

- *Les Juifs en Bretagne au XVIIIe Siècle*
- *Les Juifs de Montpellier au XVIIIe Siècle*
- *Les Juifs dans les Colonies Françaises au XVIIIe Siècle*
- *Le Trèsor des Juifs Sephardim - notes sur les familles françaises isréalites du rit portugais*
- *Inscriptions Hèbraïques d'Arles*
- *Jacob Backofen, rabbin de Metz*
- *La douane de Lyon et les juifs*
- *Marchands juifs en 1670*
- *Concile d'Orléans et les relations entre juifs et chrétiens (mariages)*

Some articles continue through many issues and really are books. All quote their sources and, if the sources are in the archives, give the facility and the code. Articles are not only in French. Many are in German, some in English, some in Hebrew, some in Italian. Nor is the subject matter limited to France.

It is those that are in French, however, that seem to contain more information that can help the genealogist. Correspondence and many other documents are copied in full. In at least one article a complete list of names from a census is given. Individual court cases are described. People's lives are explored in detail. For those who cannot travel to France to use her many archives to research their French Jewish genealogy, this publication can be a gift indeed.

The *Revue* can be found around the Internet. For ease of use, we prefer to use the Index to the first fifty volumes via the Internet Archive. It is an excellent index, with headings for both authors and subjects. Thus, just looking up a city, such as Bordeaux or Lyon, or a region, such as Lorraine, will give a list of articles. Then, we go to Scribd, where the wonderful folks at Patrologia, bless them, have uploaded all the early volumes of the *Revue*.

Enjoy!

Links:

Wikipedia has an article on the *Revue* here:
https://en.wikipedia.org/wiki/Revue_des_%C3%89tudes_Juives

You can read the index to older issues of the *Revue* on the Internet Archive:
https://archive.org/details/revuedestudesj00soci/page/n3/mode/2up?view=theater

Older issues can be found on SCRIBD:
https://www.scribd.com/search?query=Revue+des+%C3%A9tudes+juives.+1880.

You can read recent copies, for a price, at Peeters Online Journals:
https://poj.peeters-leuven.be/content.php?url=journal&journal_code=REJ

Learn more about Patrologia:
http://plgo.org/

A Useful Biographical Dictionary

Not so long ago, we trashed certain biographical publications as useless for genealogy. This is most definitely not one of them. The *Dictionnaire biographique des rabbins et autres ministres du culte israélite du Grand Sanhédrine (1808) à la loi de séparation (1905)* is a mouthful of a title for a truly fine piece of scholarship.

A joint effort between the *Commission Française des archives juives* and the *Archives nationales*, this work attempts to list every rabbi of 19th century France, including Alsace-Lorraine and the then colony of Algeria. There are over 2800 names, some with photographs of the individual, nearly all with a biographical article about him. The documentation of each entry, as one would expect from the National Archives, is impeccable, and includes information from civil registrations, education records, other religious and family records, and records of associations.

For anyone researching French Jewish ancestry, this book is valuable not only for those seeking to know more about a particular rabbi, but for those who wish to trace a family which included a rabbi and those wishing to follow rabbinical traditions in a certain locale. A serious and very useful work indeed.

The last time we checked, it was available on Abebooks.com.

Bulletin de l'Alliance Israélite Universelle

The *Alliance Israélite Universelle (AIU)* is an international organisation founded in France in 1860, after a period of nasty anti-Semitism and a celebrated case of the forced conversion of a child to Christianity. The goal of the founder, Adolphe Crémieux, was to encourage education -- with an emphasis on the idealism of the French Revolution -- for all Jewish people. The AIU has been building schools for Jewish children all over the world -- particularly in North Africa -- for the past 150 years, more than twenty years longer than the Alliance Française. It was the first international Jewish organisation and has had significant influence. A history of the AIU, edited by André Kaspi, entitled plainly *Histoire de l'Alliance israélite universelle de 1860 à nos jours*, was published in 2010.

From its beginning until the First World War, the AIU published the *Bulletin de l'Alliance Israélite Universelle* which, because it listed so many of its members and their contributions, is of enormous value in French Jewish genealogy, as described by the National Library of Israel:

"The Bulletin is also a rich source of information on the inner lives of the Jewish communities. Every issue contains detailed lists of AIU members in every city, continuous information reported from local committees spread over five continents, lists of donors or people who contributed to solidarity activities initiated by the Alliance for the benefit of Jews who had fallen victim to misfortune or violence, and more. Statistical data on the AIU schools provide accurate information about the number of schools in each city, the number of students, the make-up of the teaching staff, and the schools' budgets."

Until recently, the only way to read the *Bulletin* was to visit the library of the AIU in Paris, one of its schools around the world, or a library that has maintained a collection of it. Now, it is available online at the abovementioned National Library of Israel under its category "Historical Jewish Press", or you can just enter the title into the search box. The description and search pages are in Hebrew, English or French. The indexing is quite good. As there are so many lists of names, the results are usually many and some search refinement is required. Even so, it will be a slog through many pages, but could be a happy one for the genealogist.

Links:

Alliance Israélite Universelle (AIU)
https://www.aiu.org/fr

Alliance française
https://www.alliancefr.org/en/

National Library of Israel :
https://www.nli.org.il/en

Cercle de Généalogie Juive

We attended the *Grand Salon de Généalogie, Histoire, Patrimoine à Lunéville* and made an excellent discovery. Alsace and Lorraine have and have had a large Jewish community, so the presence of the *Cercle de Généalogie Juive* at the event was most sensible and welcome. Their table exhibiting all of their publications was fascinating. Of particular interest to some of our Dear Readers will be the book on Sephardim from the Ottoman Empire (of whom there were some eight thousand) who came to France during the First World War, *Destins de Séfarades Ottomans : les Israélites du Levant en France pendant la Première Guerre mondial,* by Philippe Denan.

Other publications include:

- Extracts from various sources on the Jewish communities of Lorraine
- Books about Jewish cemeteries throughout France, with photographs of each tombstone, transcriptions of the engravings and histories of the communities
- A regular review, "Généalo-J", produced three times per year, and which has many articles that are research guides

Many of these may be purchased from the website of the *Cercle de Généalogie Juive* as PDF documents and downloaded immediately. A complete list of the many, many publications may be found there as well.

The group is quite dynamic, with monthly lectures at the *Mémorial de la Shoah* and monthly genealogy clinics to help you with your research at the *Mediathèque du Musée d'Art et d'Histoire du Judaïsme* in Paris.

The organization is one of the best resources for French Jewish genealogy.

Links:
Cercle de Généalogie Juive :
https://www.genealoj.org/fr

Publications :
https://www.genealoj.org/fr/catalog/publications

Additional Websites

In addition to the websites mentioned above, the following also can be very helpful.

- ANOM - *Archives nationales d'Outre-Mer*
  http://www.archivesnationales.culture.gouv.fr/anom/fr/

  The Overseas Archives, these hold the archives relating to France's ex-colonies, for only the years for which they were colonies or territories. For post-colonial records, one must look in the locally based archives of that place, e.g. the National Archives of the country the colony became (such as Algeria) or the Departmental Archives, if the colony became a part of France (such as Mayotte).

  - Civil and parish registers of France's ex-colonies
  - Registers of prisoners sent to overseas penal colonies
  - A large amount of correspondence has been digitized
  - You will NOT find post-colonial records here

- Gallica - *La Bibliothèque nationale*
  https://gallica.bnf.fr/accueil/en/

  This is the website of the vast National Library of France. Explore this website, try searching a name, a company, two family names, etc. in all of the possibilities:

- o Books
- o Newspapers
- o Magazines
- o Other Publications
- o Laws
- o Images
- o Manuscripts
- o Maps

- *Mémoire des Hommes*
  https://www.memoiredeshommes.sga.defense.gouv.fr/fr/

  This is the website of history of the Armed Forces of France: the Army, the Navy, the Gendarmerie, the Marines, the Air Force, etc., called the *Service Historique de la Défense*. It has an ever-growing number of data bases of digitized information. There are now nearly thirty different sets of data, all of which can be searched at once by entering a name in the search box. Some of the more interesting are:

  - o *Base des morts en déportation* (1939-1945) This who were deported and killed during World War II
  - o *Morts Pour la France* 1914-1918 Those who died in combat in World War I
  - o *Compagnie des Indes* – France's East India Company, this database contains passenger lists.
  - o Army Muster lists of *Ancien régime* and First Empire

- *Mémorial de la Shoah*
  https://www.memorialdelashoah.org/en

> The website of the Shoah Memorial to the French victims of the Nazis, a museum and documentation centre about the people in France in the Holocaust. Click on the British flag for English.

- All Jewish Soldiers in Napoleon's Army
  https://tinyurl.com/bddnxjyu

> Someone from the French military enthusiasts' website, Ancestramil, (https://www.ancestramil.fr/cms/) uploaded, anonymously, to Google Docs a spreadsheet with the names of every Jewish soldier of the Army of the First Empire.

> It gives the full name, date of birth, parents' names, place of birth, profession, date of death, residence, and regiment WITH the file code in the military archives at the *Service Historique de la Défense.*

- AJPN - *Anonymes, Justes et persécutés durant la période nazie* (The Anonymous, Righteous and persecuted of the Nazis)
  http://www.ajpn.org/

> This remarkable website is the work of an association that says it is "committed to preserving, transmitting and teaching the history of the Second World War of each of the 36,593 municipalities of France ... with a civic approach ... comparing public archive resources, family archives and testimonies collected." The site is daily updated and currently has some 90,000 of memories and

testimonies, arranged geographically, down to the neighbourhood and street level. It is one of the best resources for first-hand accounts of the Holocaust in France.

- *Judaisme d'Alsace et de Lorraine*
  http://www.judaisme-alsalor.fr/index.htm

  This is the website of an association, filled with information about all aspects of Judaism in Alsace and Lorraine. There are songs and jokes and there are also lists of graves in cemeteries and much more to help the researcher.

- *Cartographie des enfants juifs de Paris déportés de juillet 1942 à août 1944*
  http://tetrade.huma-num.fr/Tetrademap_Enfant_Paris/

  This is the site of an interactive map showing the homes and schools of all of the Jewish children deported from Paris between July 1942 an August 1944.

www.ingramcontent.com/pod-product-compliance
Lightning Source LLC
Chambersburg PA
CBHW022127280326
41933CB00007B/580

* 9 7 9 1 0 9 6 0 8 5 1 0 1 *